3
INGREDIENT COCKTAILS

Kate Calder

INGREDIENT
COCKTAILS

Hardie Grant

BOOKS

CONTENTS

VODKA

VODKA SNACKS

GIN

GIN SNACKS

RUM

RUM SNACKS

TEQUILA

TEQUILA SNACKS

WHISKEY

WHISKEY SNACKS

SPARKLING

SPARKLING SNACKS

INTRODUCTION

I think we tend to be too nervous around cocktails – in ordering as well as preparing them. We have one or two that we know we like – safe bets – but we're reluctant to branch out and broaden our booze horizons. This book is meant to go some way towards demystifying the cocktail world and inspiring you to get mixing.

The reputation of a good cocktail is often cloaked in science and secrecy so technical and precise that mere mortals, it might seem, shouldn't even bother to try making it. It will take too long to prepare, is too fiddly – 'what if I get it wrong?'. I want to prove to you that not only does this not have to be the case, but that

for most of the world's greatest cocktails you only need three ingredients and a couple of minutes to whip them up.

Many of the classics are surrounded in legends about how they were first discovered or made. These stories are sometimes contradictory and unreliable, but there is a mythical quality to a timeless cocktail nevertheless. They are classics because they work, and there's something comforting in knowing they've been being enjoyed for decades – centuries in some cases – before we were born.

Technique is important, but it isn't everything.

Depth of flavour is a goal but getting there doesn't have to be difficult. These recipes aren't about purism or strict rules – they should inspire you to loosen up, find your flavour and customise. Here's the truth: you're not going to like all of the cocktails in this book. Everyone's tastes are different, and this is very much the case with cocktails. Whether you have a sweet tooth or a love of bitter flavours, there will be dozens of recipes in here for you, it's just a case of trying them all!

These cocktails taste amazing and don't have to be reserved for special occasions – I hope they stop you reaching for a wine or beer out of instinct! The chapters are divided by central ingredient – gin, vodka, rum, tequila, whiskey and sparkling wine – each cocktail can be made in minutes, and there are simple-to-make snack suggestions at the end of each chapter to go with them. With some new recipes, renowned classics, and batch cocktails, this book has everything you need to bring elegance, style and fun to your cocktail hour.

HAPPY DRINKING!

Kate Calder.

COCKTAILS

Since the turn of the 19th century people have been enjoying glasses of delicious concoctions to set their senses on fire. Each ingredient in a cocktail plays a vital role, starting with a base spirit for flavour, a balancing ingredient for sweetness or acidity, and a seasoning to enhance the mixture and add complexity. The most important thing to remember with cocktails is that they're for fun – so take a break from seriousness and enjoy the moment.

Cocktails should be served cold, so make sure you have freezer space and lots of ice. If you have a cocktail-shaker you're ready to go! If not, don't worry. There are many reasonably priced cocktail kits out there and you can see them as investments for life. I prefer stainless steel shakers because they get really cold, and if they slip out of your hands they stay in one piece. Others may be cute and artsy, but stainless steel means business. If you don't want to buy a shaker you can use an old jam jar, or 'mason jar'. Fill them with ice, pour the ingredients in, screw the lid on tightly and shake. For stirred recipes, put the ingredients in a jug (pitcher) full of ice and stir with a spoon.

HOW TO USE THIS BOOK

INGREDIENTS & MEASURES

The garnishes are optional extras and the drinks will taste fine without them – they just won't look as pretty, and because ice is frozen tap-water it hasn't been counted as an ingredient. All cocktail recipes listed are for making one cocktail unless otherwise stated, as in the batch recipes.

I am using 30 ml (1 fl oz) for 1 shot. Another term often used is 1 part – I found many different measurements for 1 shot, from 25 ml (0.85 fl oz) to 35 ml (1.2 fl oz). I've decided to stick with 30 ml (1 fl oz) because if you don't have a shot glass, you can use 2 tablespoons, because 1 tablespoon is 15 ml ($^{1}/_{2}$ fl oz). Saying that, you're likely to have a shot glass lurking around your kitchen. During my research I have found that a lot of cocktail recipes write in ounces, 1 ounce is 1 shot and 1 ounce is 30 ml. Many classics are easy to remember because they are simple ratios, for example a Negroni is 1:1:1. That's 1 part gin, 1 part Campari and 1 part sweet vermouth. To conclude, I chose 1 part to be 30 ml (1 fl oz) and if you have a shot glass that doesn't have millilitre measurements on it, just pretend it's 30 ml (1 fl oz), so 1 shot glass full is 30 ml (1 fl oz).

ICE

Have lots of freezer space because cocktails are meant to be very cold. I was pleasantly surprised to see crushed ice is now readily available at my local supermarket – you no longer need to bring out the food processor or beg the fishmonger for a bag.

GLASSWARE

It may sound silly, but get glassware you love and don't lock it away or keep it purely for display. Using it will, in itself, make the end product feel special.

Martini and coupe glasses should be chilled prior to pouring cocktails into them. An easy way to do this is to fill them with ice while you make the drink and then put the ice into the next glass that's going to be used or back in the freezer.

SYRUPS

A few of the recipes call for flavoured or simple syrup, also called sugar syrup. Simple syrup is available to buy at supermarkets and online (or you can use agave syrup). To make your own, take equal measures of sugar and water brought to a boil together and then cooled completely. Flavoured syrups can be found in supermarkets and online.

SNACKS

The recipes for snacks are designed to allow you to hold your cocktail with one hand and eat with the other. They are a step beyond putting out bowls of olives and crisps (chips) but they're deceptively simple. These snacks are easy to make and will impress your guests. I have matched the food with the cocktails that would complement them most, but by no means do you have to stick to that. Also, it's always a good idea to line your guests' stomachs for a long night ahead!

GLASS GLOSSARY

Cocktails are served in all sorts of glassware but don't get too hung up on owning the correct, traditional type. The good news is that mixologists have thrown a lot of which-drink-is-supposed-to-be-served-in-which-glass out of the window in recent years. Take the classic Martini as an example – once it was only ever seen in Martini glasses, but it's frequently served in lowball or coupe glasses now. This is a description of the glasses I have used in this book, as well as which cocktails they are most commonly used for, and I have also noted which glasses you can use instead if you don't have the one mentioned

1. COUPE

Once reserved for Champagne but now commonly used for Martinis and shaken cocktails as well. They have a glamorous feel, reminiscent of the Roaring Twenties and the silver screen. Not many people own coupes these days, so, instead, you can use a flute if the cocktail includes sparkling wine, or if it's a mixed drink, use a martini glass, small wine glass glass or lowball glass.

2. LOWBALL

This can also be called a tumbler, a rocks glass or an old-fashioned glass. Most people use them for spirits poured over ice or mixed cocktails high in alcoholic volume. You can use any of your kitchen's smaller glasses as a lowball, or, if you don't have small glasses, use whatever you do have, half-filled with ice.

3. MARTINI

The most iconic of glassware for cocktails, it has a classic V-shape with a long stem. It's a beautiful design, but it's also functional – the stem prevents the drinker from holding the glass itself and warming the drink with their hand. Martinis can also be served in coupes and lowball glasses, the only rule is that they must be served very cold.

4. HIGHBALL

Cylindrical, tall and flat-bottomed. They are used for cocktails with an alcohol base but a larger proportion of a non-alcoholic mixer, usually carbonated. As with the lowball, any drinking glass you have in your kitchen will work instead.

5. TIKI MUG

I wish we all had tiki mugs, but the fact is that very few of us do – you can use a highball instead.

6. LARGE WINE GLASS

I'm pretty certain if you're buying this book you will have a wine glass kicking around. Cocktails served in wine glasses are better in the larger-sized variety because cocktails are mixed drinks with multiple ingredients and ice. If you don't have a large wine glass, use the kind you do have, or a lowball.

7. FLUTE

Designed for sparkling wine, it concentrates the aromas of the wine, allows you to see the bubbles rise to the top and slows the speed at which the wine goes flat. If you are flute-less, use a small wine glass or coupe.

8. HURRICANE

Based on the shape of hurricane vases and lamps, this glass is used to serve large-volume mixed cocktails. Although they are taller and wider than highball glasses, it's perfectly fine to use a highball glass as a substitute.

9. MASON JAR

Hugely popular in BBQ season, these glass jars – jam jars by another name – are used for mixed drinks with ice and are often served with straws. There is no need to start eating more jam – you can use lowballs, highballs and wine glasses instead.

10. MARGARITA

This glass is really only used for margaritas and other beach-side bar cocktails. It's like a coupe but double-bowled and wider. Nowadays margaritas tend to be served in many other types of glass – from lowballs to mason jars.

11. MILKSHAKE GLASS

Quite retro but still popular at seaside bars, this glass is tall with a thick, curvy, ribbed design. It's great for serving heavier drinks in. Highballs and pint glasses are excellent substitutes.

12. COPPER MUG

A Moscow Mule's signature glassware that can also be used for variations on the cocktail. The copper takes on the cold temperature of the Mule but it is perfectly acceptable to serve this family of cocktails in lowballs and highballs as well.

COCKTAIL KIT

These essentials will make your cocktail evenings a little easier – but by no means are they must-haves for these recipes. I've included utensils that you will probably have in your kitchen which you can use instead

1 SHAKER

This is the container that's used to mix ingredients in. It comes with a fitted lid and strainer so you can fill the shaker with ice, then add your ingredients, and shake hard until the drink gets really cold. Remove the top lid and pour. If you don't have a shaker you can use an old food jar with its lid on, or, if the recipe calls for a stirred drink, use any jug (pitcher) or large drinking glass.

2 STRAINER

This is used to remove the ice from a mixture when pouring it into a glass. It fits into the wide mouth of the container the cocktail was prepared in and, like a sieve, it has small holes to let the liquid through but blocks the ice cubes. You could also use a large spoon to hold your ice cubes back.

3 LONG STIRRING SPOON

When a cocktail is stirred and not shaken, you need a tool to do the stirring for you. Commonly known as a swizzle stick, it needs to be long and thin to fit to the bottom of your container through the ice. Stirring helps to chill and mix the cocktail. A chopstick makes a good alternative.

4 JIGGER

This is a fancy name for a cocktail-measuring-cup that has the measurements for shots ranging from 15 ml (1/2 fl oz) to 60 ml (2 fl oz). You could use a shot glass or an egg cup instead, as these hold approximately 30 ml (1 fl oz), but if you need to be more precise use measuring spoons.

5 MUDDLER

A much-loved tool of bartenders, muddlers are used to extract flavours and aromas from herbs and fruit as well as for combining sugar, particularly sugar cubes, into cocktails. The trick is not to smash your ingredients with force but more to press down gently and give a small twist, releasing and repeating the action a few more times. If a cocktail is muddled too vigorously it will taste bitter. The end of a wooden spoon or rolling pin will work well instead.

Add a couple of reusable cocktail sticks and straws – and why not throw in a packet of cocktail umbrellas for those Tiki nights!

The most versatile of spirits, vodka complements an incredible array of flavours, from tomato juice to espresso. In the following recipes I've tried to cover the whole taste spectrum. There's not much you can't do with this beautiful, crystal-clear spirit. Vodka's worldwide popularity is due to its ability to vary in character and style. In many countries it's still enjoyed mostly in the traditional way – neat. The vodka cocktail wasn't actually introduced until 1911 in the US. The only rule is that it should be served very cold. The colder it is, the better it tastes. I keep my vodka in the freezer, always ready for action.

HAIL MARY

A savoury cocktail often used as a cure for hangovers, the Bloody Mary is a very popular brunch cocktail. Being Canadian, my favourite version is called a Caesar, which uses a clam and tomato juice. For this Hail Mary I have left out the original's call for hot sauce and horseradish and used a spicy tomato juice – a cheat's way of getting all those flavours in at once. You can really go to town in garnishing this cocktail. In Canada, there's competition between bars to see who can get the most in a glass. I've seen everything from beef jerky to chicken wings precariously balanced on the side.

- 30 ML (1 FL OZ) VODKA
- 3 DASHES OF WORCESTERSHIRE SAUCE
- 100 ML (3½ FL OZ/SCANT ½ CUP) SPICY TOMATO JUICE

METHOD
Fill your highball glass generously with ice. Pour in the vodka and add the dashes of Worcestershire sauce. Top up with tomato juice, stir well and serve.

GARNISH
Garnish with a stick of celery, a large prawn (shrimp), a lemon wedge and rim with celery salt.

RUBY SLIPPER

This cocktail is delicately sweet and very refreshing. The soda's bubbles engage your senses and lift the Chambord's raspberry flavour. Serving it in jam (mason) jars adds a bit of sweet fun to the occasion.

- 30 ML (1 FL OZ) VODKA
- 30 ML (1 FL OZ) CHAMBORD
- 100 ML (3½ FL OZ/SCANT ½ CUP) SODA WATER (CLUB SODA), OR ENOUGH TO TOP UP

METHOD
Fill your mason jar with ice and pour in the vodka and Chambord. Top up with soda, stir and serve.

GARNISH
Garnish with raspberries and edible flowers.

VIPER

'Snake in the grass' is the phrase that comes to mind for this cocktail. The sweetness of the lime, the coolness of the vodka and the tartness of the cider are an enticing mix for this wicked-witch's brew.

- 60 ML (2 FL OZ/¼ CUP) VODKA
- 15 ML (½ FL OZ/1 TABLESPOON) LIME CORDIAL
- 100 ML (3½ FL OZ/SCANT ½ CUP) DRY (HARD) CIDER

METHOD
Add a handful of ice to a large wine glass. Pour in all of the ingredients, stir and serve.

GARNISH
Garnish with slices of apple and lime.

WHITE RUSSIAN

Despite the name, this cocktail has nothing to do with Russia other than vodka being one of the ingredients. It reminds me of the film The Big Lebowski and The Dude's love of them. I must say I totally agree with him, they are utterly delicious.

- 30 ML (1 FL OZ) VODKA
- 30 ML (1 FL OZ) COFFEE LIQUEUR
- 30 ML (1 FL OZ) DOUBLE (HEAVY) CREAM

METHOD

Add a handful of ice cubes to a tumbler glass. First pour in the coffee liqueur, followed by the vodka and then the double cream. Whether you stir it or not is up to you. Serve.

GARNISH

No garnish.

APPLE PIE

Vodka complements the classic and familiar combination of apple and cinnamon perfectly because it doesn't overpower their flavours but enhances them. This is a cosy drink that, despite being served on ice, is like a big hug in a glass.

- 60 ML (2 FL OZ/¼ CUP) VODKA
- 15 ML (½ FL OZ/1 TABLESPOON) CINNAMON SYRUP
- 75 ML (2½ FL OZ) CLOUDY APPLE JUICE

METHOD

Fill your tumbler glass with ice and pour in the vodka and cinnamon syrup. Top up with apple juice, stir and serve.

GARNISH

Garnish with ground cinnamon sprinkled on top.

MOSCOW MULE

Legend has it that a barman in New York came up with the Moscow Mule when he was clearing out the unused ginger beer and vodka from his cellar. The cocktail quickly became popular across the United States in the mid-20th century. It is almost always served in a copper mug because it takes on the cold temperature of the cocktail.

> PICTURED ON PAGE 35 <

- 60 ML (2 FL OZ/¼ CUP) VODKA
- 2 LIMES, JUICED
- 100 ML (3½ FL OZ/SCANT ½ CUP) GINGER BEER, OR ENOUGH TO TOP UP

METHOD

Fill your Moscow mule mug or highball glass to the top with crushed ice. Pour in the vodka and lime juice. Top up with ginger beer, stir well and serve.

GARNISH

Garnish with wedges of lime and sprigs of mint.

ESPRESSO MARTINI

One of my favourite cocktails, this is the perfect drink to kick off a night's celebrations — or to keep the night going! Prepare the espresso beforehand, then chill it in the fridge until it's really cold. This will develop its depth of flavour and make it even more delicious. I don't have an espresso machine at home, so I use an intense-rated ground coffee and follow the packet instructions (essentially, I just make a really strong cup of coffee and chill it in the fridge for a few hours and it works brilliantly).

- 60 ML (2 FL OZ/¼ CUP) VODKA
- 30 ML (1 FL OZ) COFFEE LIQUEUR
- 30 ML (1 FL OZ) CHILLED ESPRESSO

METHOD
Fill your cocktail shaker with ice and then add all of the ingredients. Secure the lid and shake vigorously for 20 seconds. Strain into your martini glass and serve.

GARNISH
Garnish with a slice of Stroopwaffle.

LEMON DROP

This delicious sweet treat of a cocktail will flood you with childhood memories of trips to your favourite sweet shop (candy store). It's often found as a shot at uni and college bars around the world, but I would argue that using fresh lemon juice and sipping it from a long, stemmed glass gives this cocktail the elegance it deserves.

- 60 ML (2 FL OZ/¼ CUP) VODKA
- 30 ML (1 FL OZ) LEMON JUICE
- 30 ML (1 FL OZ) SIMPLE SUGAR SYRUP

METHOD
Fill your cocktail shaker with ice and then add all of the ingredients. Secure the lid and shake vigorously for 20 seconds. Strain into your coupe glass and serve.

GARNISH
Garnish with a sugar rim or crush some boiled lemon sweets (hard candies) and use them to dip the rim into instead.

SAKE-TINI

Japanese sake is a light, smooth rice wine that is very popular around the world. It works incredibly well in gin and vodka martinis instead of dry vermouth. Mixing it with vodka and Cointreau gives a delicate, refreshing and sophisticated cocktail that could easily become your new favourite.

- 60 ML (2 FL OZ/¼ CUP) VODKA
- 30 ML (1 FL OZ) SAKE
- 15 ML (½ FL OZ/1 TABLESPOON) COINTREAU

METHOD
Fill your cocktail shaker with ice and then add all of the ingredients. Secure the lid and shake vigorously for 20 seconds. Strain into your martini glass and serve.

GARNISH
Garnish with a twist of grapefruit peel and a cucumber ribbon secured on a cocktail stick.

CITRUS PUNCH

Punchy, sweet cocktails for serving a crowd, punch bowls were made for cocktails like this one. The ginger beer and vodka pairing lifts the fruit juice and makes it invigorating.

- 30 ML (1 FL OZ) VODKA
- 60 ML (2 FL OZ/¼ CUP) CITRUS FRUIT JUICE
- 60 ML (2 FL OZ/¼ CUP) ALCOHOLIC GINGER BEER

BATCH TO SERVE 4

- 100 ML (3½ FL OZ/SCANT ½ CUP) VODKA
- 250 ML (8½ FL OZ/1 CUP) CITRUS FRUIT JUICE
- 250 ML (8½ FL OZ/1 CUP) ALCOHOLIC GINGER BEER

METHOD

Fill a highball glass with ice and pour in the vodka and fruit juice. Top up with ginger beer, stir and serve.

For a batch, add all of the ingredients to a pouring jug (pitcher), or punch bowl with ice, stir and serve.

GARNISH

Garnish with an orange, lemon and lime sunset.

VODKA
SNACKS

→

Most vodka is made in cold, slavic nations, and for that reason is often paired with those countries' pickled, smoked and cured foods. But I'd argue that because vodka is very versatile when it comes to cocktails, the same holds true when matching food with it. It does work perfectly with savoury acidic dishes like pickles, that's true, but it works equally well with decadent, rich chocolate desserts.

DILL & SESAME PICKLED CUCUMBERS

I love the art of pickling but I am also impatient. These are super-quick and give you the same kick as if they had been pickled for days!

INGREDIENTS

- 1 CUCUMBER OR 5 MINI CUCUMBERS, CUT INTO 10-CM (4-IN) SPEARS
- 1 TEASPOON SALT
- 2 TEASPOONS TAMARIND PASTE
- 1 TEASPOON SESAME OIL
- 2 TEASPOONS SUGAR
- 100 ML (3$\frac{1}{2}$ FL OZ/SCANT $\frac{1}{2}$ CUP) WHITE WINE VINEGAR
- SMALL HANDFUL OF FRESH DILL, CHOPPED
- 1 TEASPOON ROASTED SESAME SEEDS

METHOD

Put the spears into a bowl and toss with the salt to evenly coat each spear. Chill in the fridge for 10 minutes. Meanwhile, mix the rest of the ingredients, except the fresh dill and sesame seeds, in a measuring jug (pitcher), until the sugar has dissolved.

Pour the vinegar mixture over the salted cucumbers and stir. Chill for another 10 minutes or until serving. Serve the spears on a plate, with a little of the pickling juice spooned over and the dill and sesame seeds sprinkled on top.

VEGETARIAN | MAKES APPROXIMATELY 24

CHOCOLATE & SALT COOKIES

'Cookies?!' you say. Absolutely. For the sweet-toothed of the party, or to serve with an end-of-night cocktail, these really hit the spot.

45 MINS

INGREDIENTS

- 110 G (4 OZ/7³/₄ TABLESPOONS) UNSALTED BUTTER, ROOM TEMPERATURE
- 100 G (3¹/₂ OZ/SCANT ¹/₂ CUP) CASTER (GRANULATED) SUGAR
- 100 G (3¹/₂ OZ/GENEROUS ¹/₂ CUP) LIGHT BROWN SUGAR
- 1 EGG
- ¹/₂ TEASPOON VANILLA EXTRACT
- ¹/₄ TEASPOON ALMOND EXTRACT
- 225 G (8 OZ/GENEROUS 1³/₄ CUPS) PLAIN (ALL-PURPOSE) FLOUR
- ¹/₂ TEASPOON BAKING POWDER
- ¹/₂ TEASPOON BICARBONATE OF SODA (BAKING SODA)
- 100 G (3¹/₂ OZ) DARK (BITTERSWEET) CHOCOLATE, CHOPPED INTO SMALL CHUNKS
- 2 LARGE PINCHES OF SEA SALT FLAKES

METHOD

Using an electric whisk, beat the butter and both sugars until smooth (about 1 minute). Add the egg, vanilla and almond extracts, and, using a spatula, mix until smooth. Add the flour, baking powder and bicarbonate of soda and mix until combined. Stir in the chocolate chunks. Chill for 15 minutes.

Heat the oven to 190°C (375°F/gas 5). Using a tablespoon, scoop the dough out into balls, and place evenly across 2–3 baking sheets lined with baking parchment. Sprinkle a little salt onto each cookie. Bake for 10 minutes or until browning at the edges. Serve straight away with another sprinkling of salt or leave to cool on a wire rack and store in an airtight container until ready to serve.

MAKES APPROXIMATELY 16

SLOW COOKED CHERRY TOMATOES, BACON & GARLIC MAYO IN LETTUCE CUPS

A BLT is my favourite sandwich, and I could eat it for breakfast, lunch and dinner. Take the bread away and you have a light, crunchy snack that won't fill you up but which still has all the flavour.

35 MINS

INGREDIENTS

- 400 G (14 OZ) CHERRY TOMATOES
- 1 TABLESPOON OLIVE OIL
- 1 TABLESPOON BALSAMIC VINEGAR
- 100 ML (3½ FL OZ/SCANT ½ CUP) MAYONNAISE
- 1 GARLIC CLOVE, CRUSHED
- ½ LEMON, JUICED
- 6 RASHERS (SLICES) OF STREAKY BACON
- 2 LITTLE GEM (BIBB) LETTUCE, LEAVES SEPARATED
- SALT

METHOD

Heat the oven to 180°C (350°F/gas 4). Line a lipped baking sheet or shallow roasting pan with baking parchment. Spread the cherry tomatoes out in an even layer and drizzle over the oil and vinegar. Sprinkle with a large pinch of salt. Roast for 30 minutes.

Meanwhile, mix the mayonnaise with the garlic and lemon juice and set aside. In a wide frying pan (skillet), lay out the bacon evenly and cook until brown and crispy on each side. Remove onto paper towels to drain the excess fat, then roughly chop.

To serve, lay out the lettuce cups and put a dollop of the mayonnaise mixture into each. Add 2–4 roasted tomatoes in each cup, top with crispy bacon bits and serve.

Both timeless and ever-more fashionable, gin is the cornerstone of many classic cocktails. The term 'cocktail', for most people, usually conjures the image of a sophisticated dry Gin Martini with an olive – it is very much part of pop culture. Aromas of juniper, citrus and coriander (cilantro) swirl around to give it balance that lends itself to mixing easily with other fresh, bold flavours and to pairing well with many foods. Sometimes only a splash of gin is needed to shape the dynamic of the cocktail, or in the case of the Martini little else is required.

ICE 'N' SPICY

A spicy twist on a classic G & T. The addition of the sweet and woody cinnamon flavour is subtle but could well make this your new favourite long drink.

- 60 ML (2 FL OZ/¼ CUP) GIN
- 100 ML (3½ FL OZ/SCANT ½ CUP) TONIC WATER, OR ENOUGH TO TOP UP
- 15 ML (½ FL OZ/1 TABLESPOON) CINNAMON SYRUP

METHOD

Fill your highball glass generously with ice. Pour in the gin then top up with tonic water. Finish by pouring in the syrup, stir well and serve.

GARNISH

Garnish with a ground cinnamon rim on the glass, a cinnamon stick and a slice of orange.

GIMLET

The hero's cocktail of choice in endless films noir, it's a drink you've probably heard of but most likely have never tried. It's time to fix this – it's like key lime pie in a glass – totally dreamy.

- 60 ML (2 FL OZ/¼ CUP) GIN
- 50 ML (1¾ FL OZ) LIME JUICE
- 30 ML (1 FL OZ) SIMPLE SUGAR SYRUP

METHOD

Fill a shaker with ice and pour in all the ingredients. Secure the lid and shake vigorously for 20 seconds, then strain into your coupe glass and serve.

GARNISH

Garnish with a sugar-dipped slice of lime.

ANTIOXIDANT

The addition of gin somewhat undoes the health benefits of the pomegranate juice of course, but I think you can still feel a tad superior when mixing this. It also looks and tastes incredible.

- 60 ML (2 FL OZ/¼ CUP) GIN
- 60 ML (2 FL OZ/¼ CUP) POMEGRANATE JUICE
- 100 ML (3½ FL OZ/SCANT ½ CUP) TONIC WATER, OR ENOUGH TO TOP UP

METHOD
Fill your highball glass generously with ice. Pour in the gin and pomegranate juice. Top up with tonic, stir well and serve.

GARNISH
Garnish with pomegranate seeds or a wedge of pomegranate.

PINK LADY

Pretty, flirty and fun, this cocktail is deceptively easy to drink and could get you into loads of trouble, so drink up!

- 60 ML (2 FL OZ/¼ CUP) GIN
- 15 ML (½ FL OZ/1 TABLESPOON) GRENADINE
- 1 EGG WHITE

METHOD

Put all the ingredients in a cocktail shaker. Secure the lid and shake vigorously for 20 seconds. Add 2 handfuls of ice cubes to the shaker. Shake for 20 seconds more. Strain into your coupe glass and serve.

GARNISH

Garnish with strawberry sweets (foam candies).

FIRE ON ICE

Kick-start the evening with this cocktail – it manages to be incredibly refreshing as well as warming.

- 60 ML (2 FL OZ/¼ CUP) GIN
- 30 ML (1 FL OZ) GINGER SYRUP
- 50 ML (1¾ FL OZ) SODA WATER (CLUB SODA), OR ENOUGH TO TOP UP THE GLASS

METHOD

Fill your tumbler glass with crushed ice. Pour in all of the ingredients and stir for 20 seconds. Add more ice and top up with more soda water.

GARNISH

Garnish with a slice of fresh ginger.

SLOE BUCK

Sloe gin is in need of a renaissance. It is a beautiful and underused spirit. This delicious spin on a Buck's Fizz is much more complex and rewarding. Be warned, it goes down almost too easily.

- 30 ML (1 FL OZ) SLOE GIN
- 30 ML (1 FL OZ) ORANGE JUICE
- 100 ML (3½ FL OZ/SCANT ½ CUP) SPARKLING WINE

METHOD
Pour the sloe gin and orange juice into your flute glass, then top up with bubbles and serve.

GARNISH
Garnish with orange zest.

NEGRONI

The bold Italian count of cocktails. A perfect balance of fragrant, bitter and sweet. This quintessential combination not only tastes incredible but is ridiculously easy to make.

- 30 ML (1 FL OZ) GIN, PREFERABLY PLYMOUTH GIN
- 30 ML (1 FL OZ) CAMPARI
- 30 ML (1 FL OZ) SWEET VERMOUTH

METHOD

Add ice to your tumbler glass and set aside. Fill a shaker with ice and pour in all the ingredients. Stir for 20 seconds, then strain into the glass and serve with ice.

GARNISH

Garnish with a thick orange twist.

GIN RICKEY

Obviously only one ingredient separates this from its far more popular cousin (see page 121). But the difference that switching tonic to soda makes is amazing. Incredibly light and refreshing, this is a real thirst-quencher.

> PICTURED ON PAGE 60 <

- 60 ML (2 FL OZ/¼ CUP) GIN
- 15 ML (½ FL OZ/1 TABLESPOON) LIME JUICE
- 100 ML (3½ FL OZ/SCANT ½ CUP) OF SODA WATER (CLUB SODA), OR ENOUGH TO TOP UP

METHOD

Fill your highball glass generously with ice. Pour in the gin and lime juice. Top up with the soda water, stir well and serve.

GARNISH

Garnish with a wedge of lime.

SUMMER STROLL

This is the English countryside in a highball glass. It's the perfect cocktail for days spent outside, whether as an accompaniment to a barbecue or to pretending you understand or care about the rules of cricket.

- 60 ML (2 FL OZ/½ CUP) GIN
- 30 ML (1 FL OZ) ELDERFLOWER CORDIAL
- 100 ML (3½ FL OZ/SCANT ½ CUP) SODA WATER (CLUB SODA), OR ENOUGH TO TOP UP

BATCH TO SERVE 4

- 250 ML (8 ½ FL OZ/1 CUP) GIN
- 150 ML (5 FL OZ/SCANT ⅔ CUP) ELDERFLOWER CORDIAL
- 500 ML (17 FL OZ/2 CUPS) SODA WATER (CLUB SODA)

METHOD

Fill your highball glass generously with ice. Pour in the gin and cordial. Top up with soda, stir well and serve.

For a batch, add all of the ingredients to a pouring jug (pitcher) or punch bowl with ice, stir and serve.

GARNISH

Garnish with edible flowers and slices of lemon and kiwi fruit.

DIRTY MARTINI

In my opinion, the addition of brine makes a martini more accessible and less intimidating (for the classic version simply remove the olive brine). If you prefer vodka, substitute that for gin but use the same measurements.

- 60 ML GIN (2 FL OZ/¼ CUP)
- 15 ML (½ FL OZ/1 TABLESPOON) DRY VERMOUTH
- 15 ML (½ FL OZ/1 TABLESPOON) OLIVE BRINE

METHOD

Fill a shaker with ice and pour in all the ingredients. Secure the lid and shake vigorously for 20 seconds and then strain into your martini glass and serve.

GARNISH

Garnish with an olive.

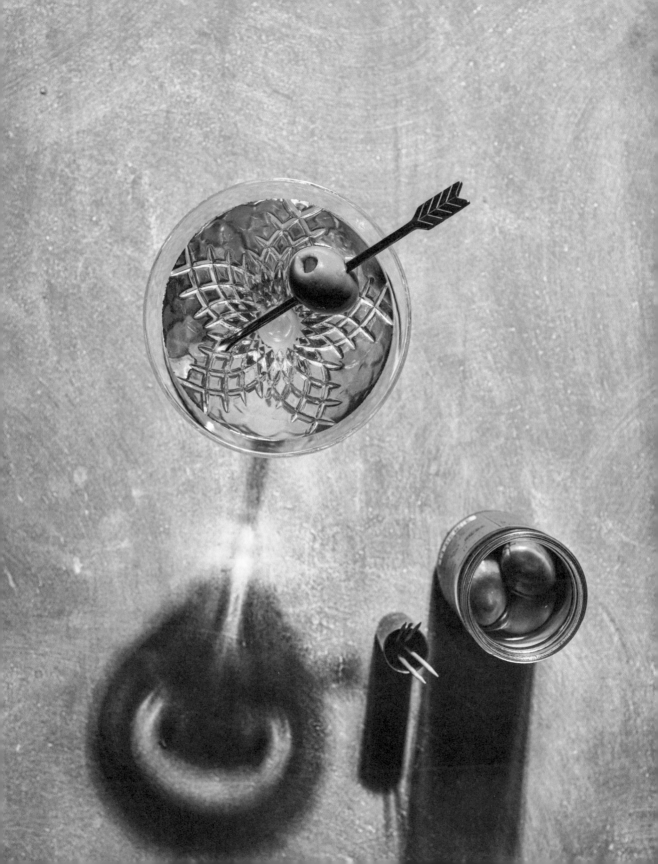

GIN
SNACKS

⟫———————▶

Taking one step up from obvious, traditional accompaniments to gin like cucumber sandwiches and prawn (shrimp) cocktail (still stone-cold classics to my eyes), here are three deceptively easy but moreish snacks to pair with this spirit. Cheese and cured meats are excellently salty and savoury ingredients that will cut through the sweetness of some gin cocktails, but which also complement gin's botanical makeup.

SWEET POTATO BITES WITH CHORIZO, SPRING ONION & SPICY MAYO

This combination is so tasty and addictive. Chorizo is one of those ingredients that will always make a dish better, from salad to stew. These are effortless to make and look really professional.

35 MINS

INGREDIENTS

- 2 LARGE SWEET POTATOES (350 G/12 OZ) PEELED AND CUT INTO 1-CM (½-IN) ROUNDS, THE LARGER ONES INTO ½ MOONS
- 1 TABLESPOON OLIVE OIL
- A LARGE PINCH OF SALT
- 1 X 200 G (7 OZ) CHORIZO SAUSAGE RING, CUT INTO 5 MM (¼-IN) ROUNDS – IF THE SAUSAGE IS IN A TOUGH CASING, THEN PEEL IT OFF BEFORE COOKING
- 2 SPRING ONIONS (SCALLIONS), CHOPPED
- 2 TABLESPOONS MAYONNAISE
- 1 TEASPOON SRIRACHA OR ANY OTHER HOT SAUCE

METHOD

Heat the oven to 200°C (400°F/gas 6). In a bowl, toss the sweet potatoes with the olive oil and salt. Line a baking sheet with baking parchment and arrange the sweet potato in a single layer. Bake for 20 minutes or until the potatoes are cooked through and browning at the edges.

Over a medium heat, fry the chorizo in a pan for about 5 minutes on both sides until it becomes crispy and its oil is released. Meanwhile, in a small bowl, mix the mayonnaise with the sriracha and a teaspoon of water and set aside.

Place the potato bites on a serving platter. Add a piece of the chorizo to each bite. Scatter over the spring onions and drizzle on the spicy mayo with a spoon.

VEGETARIAN | SERVES 8

BAKED RICOTTA WITH HONEY-LEMON PEACHES & BASIL

Fruit and cheese go together in perfect harmony. This quick-to-prepare peach chutney offers a sweet and fresh twist to this classic dish.

35 MINS

INGREDIENTS

- 500 G (1 LB 2 OZ) RICOTTA
- 1 EGG
- 4 HEAPED TABLESPOONS GRATED PARMESAN
- ½ TEASPOON SALT
- FRESHLY GROUND BLACK PEPPER
- 2 TABLESPOONS OLIVE OIL
- 1 X 227-G (8-OZ) CAN OF PEACH SLICES, DRAINED AND ROUGHLY CHOPPED
- 1 TABLESPOON HONEY
- 1 SMALL LEMON, ZESTED AND JUICED
- A SMALL HANDFUL OF BASIL LEAVES, SHREDDED
- 1 BAGUETTE

METHOD

Heat the oven to 200°C (400°F/gas 6). In a large bowl, mix the ricotta with the egg, 3 heaped tablespoons of the Parmesan, the salt and a few grindings of pepper. Use 1 tablespoon of the oil to grease a baking dish (I used a 18 x 4 cm (7 x 1½ in) terracotta one), then put in the ricotta mix, spreading it out evenly. Sprinkle over the remaining Parmesan. Cook in the top third of the oven for about 30 minutes or until starting to brown on top.

Meanwhile, in a bowl, mix the peaches with the honey, lemon zest and juice, and the basil.

Cut the baguette into 1.5-cm (3/4-in) slices, put them onto a baking sheet and put in the oven for 5 minutes to toast lightly.

Remove the ricotta from the oven when it's cooked and starting to brown, drizzle over the remaining olive oil and decorate the edge with the peach mix. Serve with the toasted baguette.

VEGETARIAN | MAKES 36

SAVOURY SHORTBREAD WITH ROSEMARY, PARMESAN, WALNUTS & RED ONION

Not your average granny's shortbread, these sophisticated bites are deliciously addictive and are host-friendly because you can get ahead and make them before your guests arrive.

1 HOUR

INGREDIENTS

- 125 G (4 OZ OR ½ CUP PLUS 1 TABLESPOON SOFTENED BUTTER
- 125 G (4 OZ OR 1 CUP MINUS 1 TABLESPOON) PLAIN (ALL-PURPOSE) FLOUR
- 30 G (1 OZ OR ¼ CUP) CORNFLOUR (CORNSTARCH)
- 1 LEMON, ZESTED
- 3 TABLESPOONS GRATED PARMESAN
- 1 TABLESPOON CHOPPED ROSEMARY
- A PINCH OF SALT
- 1 SMALL RED ONION, FINELY CHOPPED
- A HANDFUL OF WALNUT HALVES, ROUGHLY CHOPPED

METHOD

With your hands, mix the butter, flour, cornflour, lemon zest, Parmesan, rosemary and salt together. Turn out onto a lightly floured work surface and, using a rolling pin, roll out until 5 mm (1/4 in) thick. It will be crumbly so don't be afraid to patch the cracks together. Using a 4–6 cm (1 1/2–2 1/4 in) fluted or star cookie cutter, stamp out 36 biscuits, re-rolling the offcuts as necessary. Decorate each biscuit with walnuts and onion.
Put the biscuits on 2 baking sheets lined with baking parchment and put in the fridge to chill for 30 minutes. Heat the oven to 180°C (350°F/gas 4) fan. Bake for 10-12 minutes or until golden at the edges. Serve straight away, or keep for the next day in an airtight container.

Originating in the West Indies in the
17th century, rum has long been synonymous
with the beach. I tend to forget how much I
love a rum cocktail – we should be enjoying
more of them at home – not waiting until we
are in our swimsuits to order them. Ideally,
I would drink every rum cocktail out of a
coconut shell, but glasses are fine as well.

CUBA LIBRE

This cocktail is named for its Cuban heritage. It mixes the tropical flavour of rum with the spicy notes of the cola and the fresh lime juice keeps it from being too sweet. Containing both caffeine and sugar, the Cuba Libre is the perfect party drink.

- 30 ML (1 FL OZ) LIGHT RUM
- 3 WEDGES OF LIME
- 120 ML (4 FL OZ/½ CUP) COLA OR ENOUGH TO TOP UP

BATCH TO SERVE 4

- 120 ML (4 FL OZ/½ CUP) LIGHT RUM
- 2 LIMES, EACH CUT INTO 6 WEDGES
- 500 ML (17 FL OZ/2 CUPS) COLA

METHOD

Fill your highball glass with ice. Pour the rum into the glass and squeeze in the limes, dropping the wedges in as you go. Add ice, top up with cola, stir and serve.

If you are making a batch, put all of the ingredients in a pouring jug (pitcher) or punch bowl with ice, stir and serve.

GARNISH

Garnish with lime wedges.

COCONUT DAIQUIRI

This is how an original Daiquiri was made before blenders conquered the world's beach-side bars. If you love coconut, you will worship this.

- 60 ML (2 FL OZ / ¼ CUP) WHITE RUM
- 30 ML (1 FL OZ) LIME JUICE
- 60 ML (2 FL OZ / ¼ CUP) COCONUT SYRUP

METHOD
Fill your cocktail shaker with ice and add all of the ingredients. Secure the lid and shake vigorously for 20 seconds. Strain into your daquiri glass and serve.

GARNISH
Garnish with a twist of lime.

BEACHCOMBER

I know adding wine to a rum cocktail sounds odd and like it shouldn't work, but it does. The wine lifts the sweetness of the rum and makes its flavour more complex and tart.

- 30 ML (1 FL OZ) DARK RUM
- 1 TEASPOON SIMPLE SUGAR SYRUP
- 50 ML (1 ¾ FL OZ) WHITE WINE

METHOD
Add ice to your tumbler glass and set aside. Fill the shaker with ice and pour in all the ingredients. Stir for 20 seconds then strain into your glass and serve.

GARNISH
Garnish with a few frozen grapes.

RUM RUNNER

A tropical cocktail found at practically every beach bar along the shores of the Pacific, it's made of the classic combination of rum and fruit. It tastes (okay, maybe just looks) better in an overly garnished Tiki mug but as it's unlikely you'll have one among the teacups, a rum runner tastes great in a highball glass too.

- 60 ML (2 FL OZ/ ¼ CUP) DARK RUM
- 100 ML (3½ FL OZ/SCANT ½ CUP) PINEAPPLE JUICE
- 1 TABLESPOON GRENADINE

METHOD

Fill your tiki glass or hurricane mug with ice and set aside. Fill your cocktail shaker with ice and then add all of the ingredients. Secure the lid and shake vigorously for 20 seconds. Strain into your mug or glass and serve.

GARNISH

Garnish with slices of pineapple, a maraschino cherry, pineapple leaves and an umbrella.

DARK FALL

These ingredients come together beautifully. The cider makes this cocktail refreshing, the rum gives it depth, and the ginger beer adds fire.

- 60 ML (2 FL OZ/¼ CUP) DARK RUM
- 100 ML (3½ FL OZ/SCANT ½ CUP) GINGER BEER
- 150 ML (5 FL OZ/SCANT ⅔ CUP) (HARD) CIDER

METHOD

Fill your mason jar or highball glass with ice and set aside. Pour in all of the ingredients. Stir and serve.

GARNISH

Garnish with red apple slices.

MOCHEATO

Purists will hate me for this recipe, but I stand by it. No, it's not the classic, much-loved Mojito, but this tastes really fresh, minty and sweet and is easy to make – and it only has three ingredients. If you don't have a muddler, you can use the end of a rolling pin.

- 60 ML (2 FL OZ/¼ CUP) WHITE RUM
- 100 ML (3½ FL OZ/SCANT ½ CUP) LEMON AND LIME SOFT DRINK
- A HANDFUL OF FRESH MINT LEAVES

METHOD

In the bottom of your highball glass, muddle the mint leaves and the rum for about 20 seconds to release the flavour of the mint. Add enough crushed ice to nearly reach the top of the glass. Pour in the lemon and lime drink and stir well. Top with more ice, if needed, and serve.

GARNISH

Garnish with lime wedges and sprigs of mint.

PIÑA COLADA

'If you like Piña Coladas...' – the lyrics from Rupert Holmes song Escape is always playing in my head when I make these. Use the type of coconut milk from a can that you use for cooking, not the beverage used for coffees. I've seen a lot of people use coconut cream in recipes, but that always curdles when I try it. I prefer a Piña Colada on the rocks, but if you have a food processor you can put all of the ingredients in with a handful of ice, whizz and enjoy the frozen version.

- 60 ML (2 FL OZ/¼ CUP) LIGHT RUM OR MALIBU RUM
- 60 ML (2 FL OZ/¼ CUP) CANNED COCONUT MILK
- 100 ML (3½ FL OZ/SCANT ½ CUP) PINEAPPLE JUICE

METHOD

Fill your hurricane or highball glass with ice and set aside. Fill your cocktail shaker with ice and then add all of the ingredients. Secure the lid and shake vigorously for 20 seconds. Strain into your glass and serve.

GARNISH

Garnish with a maraschino cherry and a slice of pineapple.

BEE'S KNEES

For an easy way to measure the mango without using scales, fill your glass to the top with frozen mango chunks and that is the amount you will need in the recipe. Leave out the rum and children will love it too.

- 30 ML (1 FL OZ) SPICED RUM
- 140 G (4¾ OZ) FROZEN MANGO CHUNKS
- 1 TABLESPOON HONEY

METHOD

Add all of the ingredients and 100 ml (3½ fl oz/scant ½ cup) of water to a food processor. Whizz for 1 minute until smooth. Pour into your tumbler glass and serve.

GARNISH

Garnish with mango slices.

BLUE HAWAIIAN

Looking at this cocktail is like gazing into the waters of the Caribbean. Blue cocktails are often smirked at and thought of as tacky, but I disagree. Curaçao is a Caribbean liqueur made from dried citrus peel and although its flavour is sweet, it is also is a little bitter, similar to triple sec.

- 30 ML (1 FL OZ) LIGHT RUM
- 30 ML (1 FL OZ) BLUE CURAÇAO LIQUEUR
- 60 ML (2 FL OZ/¼ CUP) CANNED COCONUT MILK

METHOD

Fill your cocktail shaker with ice and then add all of the ingredients. Secure the lid and shake vigorously for 20 seconds. Strain into a coupe glass and serve.

GARNISH

Garnish with an orange slice and a carnation. . .

RUMSHAKE

Originating from sugarcane, it's no wonder that rum works really well as an ingredient in many desserts. This is a really fun version of an adults-only ice-cream sundae. You will need a food processor or hand blender for this recipe.

- 60 ML (2 FL OZ/¼ CUP) RUM
- 4 SCOOPS OR 150 G (5 OZ) VANILLA ICE CREAM
- 2 STRAWBERRIES

METHOD

Add the rum and ice cream to the drum of your food processor. Whizz until smooth. Pour half into your highball or milkshake glass. Add the strawberries to the food processor and whizz again until smooth. Pour over the vanilla and serve.

GARNISH

Garnish with whipped cream, hundreds and thousands and a stripey straw.

RUM
SNACKS

$\longrightarrow$

Rum cocktails are very popular in warm climates so it's fitting that the dishes that work best with them are made with ingredients you would find on warmer shores. Bold, fresh, tropical flavours complement rum perfectly. Foods such as shellfish, citrus fruits, coconut and all the other delicious beach holiday foods you can think of are exactly what rum pairs perfectly with.

SERVES 6

CORN & PRAWN SALSA

Roll this salsa up in a soft tortilla or eat with your favourite lettuce leaves for a superb lunch.

10
MINS

INGREDIENTS

- 1 X 198-G (7-OZ) CAN OF SWEETCORN (CORN KERNELS), DRAINED AND RINSED, OR THE SLICED OFF CORN FROM TWO COOKED COBS
- 1 AVOCADO, CHOPPED
- 2 TABLESPOONS SOUR CREAM
- 1 LIME, ZESTED AND JUICED
- A HANDFUL OF CORIANDER (CILANTRO) LEAVES, ROUGHLY CHOPPED
- 1 TABLESPOON OLIVE OIL
- 200 G (7 OZ) COOKED PRAWNS (SHRIMP), LEFT WHOLE IF SMALL OR CHOPPED IF LARGE (I USED ATLANTIC PRAWNS)
- 1 GREEN CHILLI, DESEEDED AND FINELY CHOPPED
- 3 SPRING ONIONS (SCALLIONS), CHOPPED
- 1 BAG OF TORTILLA CHIPS
- SALT

METHOD

Add all of the ingredients except the tortilla chips to a shallow, wide bowl. Give everything a good stir and serve with the chips..

MAKES ABOUT 12 PIECES

STICKY HONEY GARLIC SESAME DRUMSTICKS

Make sure you have put out your cocktail napkins for this finger-licking good chicken.

1
HOUR (PLUS MARINATING)

INGREDIENTS

- 1 KG (2 LB 4 OZ) CHICKEN DRUMSTICKS
- 1 TABLESPOON CRUSHED GARLIC OR GARLIC PASTE
- 1 TABLESPOON FINELY CHOPPED GINGER OR GINGER PASTE
- 60 ML (2 FL OZ/¼ CUP) DARK SOY SAUCE
- 60 ML (2 FL OZ/¼ CUP) RUNNY HONEY
- 1 TEASPOON BROWN SUGAR
- 1 TEASPOON SESAME OIL
- 1 TEASPOON ROASTED SESAME SEEDS

METHOD

In a large bowl, add all the ingredients except the sesame seeds and stir, making sure each drumstick is covered in marinade. Leave to marinate for an hour or two.

Heat the oven to 180°C (350°F/gas 4). Line a lipped baking sheet or shallow roasting pan with baking parchment. Remove the drumsticks from the marinade and lay them out in a single layer on the tray. Spoon over the remaining marinade. Roast in the oven for 40 minutes, spooning over the marinade after 20 minutes. After 40 minutes spoon over the marinade again and then turn the oven up to 200°C (400°F/gas 6) and roast for another 20 minutes. It's okay if it starts to blacken.

Arrange the drumsticks on a serving platter, sprinkle over the sesame seeds and serve.

VEGETARIAN | SERVES 8

ROASTED LIME & COCONUT NEW POTATOES WITH A HOT YOGURT DIP

Usually an ingredient kept for desserts, coconut works wonderfully in savoury dishes – think curries. Also, I'm a big fan of bitter flavours and love roasted citrus fruit. The roasted lime gives this dish a burst of zest that will send your taste buds soaring. Make sure to stick a few cocktail sticks (toothpicks) into the potatoes and shallots, and have more on the side for guests to help themselves to.

35 MINS

INGREDIENTS

- 750 G (1 LB 10 OZ) BABY NEW POTATOES, LARGER ONES HALVED
- 2 SHALLOTS, SLICED
- 2 LIMES, 1 ZESTED AND JUICED, 1 THINLY SLICED
- 2 TABLESPOONS UNSWEETENED DESICCATED (DRIED SHREDDED) COCONUT
- 1 TABLESPOON OLIVE OIL
- 150 G (5 OZ/SCANT ⅔ CUP) PLAIN YOGURT
- 1 TEASPOON HOT SAUCE
- SALT

METHOD

Heat the oven to 200°C (400°F/gas 6). In a large bowl mix the potatoes with the shallots, the lime zest and juice as well as the sliced lime, the coconut, olive oil, and 2 large pinches of salt until evenly coated. Pour the mixture out onto a lined baking sheet in a single layer. Roast for 30 minutes or until the potatoes are cooked through. In a small serving bowl, mix the yogurt with the hot sauce and serve with the roasted lime coconut potatoes and shallots.

TEQUILA

Tequila: the go-go juice of the cocktail world. This Mexican spirit comes from the sap of the blue agave plant and has been around for centuries. It continues to inspire some of the craziest drinking stories. Our initial experiences with tequila may have been wincing over room-temperature shots at the bar but nowadays this spirit is as respected among top bartenders as whiskey and gin, and forms the base of a growing number of sophisticated cocktails.

OL' SMOKEY

Like tequila, mezcal is made in Mexico and is hundreds, perhaps even thousands, of years old, but only received its Denominación de Origin status in 2005. It has a smokey flavour and, in Mexico, it is often drunk straight, served alongside slices of lime, lemon and orange sprinkled with salt, chilli pepper and ground fried larvae! If you're a margarita fan you will love this just as much.

- 30 ML (1 FL OZ) TEQUILA
- 15 ML (½ FL OZ/1 TABLESPOON) MEZCAL
- 100 ML (3½ FL OZ/SCANT ½ CUP) PINK GRAPEFRUIT JUICE

METHOD

Fill your tumbler glass with ice and set aside. Fill your cocktail shaker with ice, then add all of the ingredients. Secure the lid and shake vigorously for 20 seconds. Strain into your glass and serve.

GARNISH

Garnish with grapefruit slices and a salted rim.

TEQUILA SUNRISE

Do not over-stir this cocktail! You want to see the distinct colours to show why it's named after the rising sun. This classic had its heyday in the heady rock'n'roll haze of the 1970s. It isn't the most refined drink, but it still holds up as a refreshing and very enjoyable beverage.

- 15 ML (½ FL OZ/1 TABLESPOON) GRENADINE
- 100 ML (3½ FL OZ/SCANT ½ CUP) ORANGE JUICE
- 60 ML (2 FL OZ/¼ CUP) REPOSADO TEQUILA

METHOD
Fill your highball glass with ice and pour in the grenadine followed by the orange juice. Finish by pouring in the tequila. Give the cocktail a small stir and serve.

GARNISH
Garnish with an orange slice, maraschino cherry and a cocktail umbrella.

EL DIABLO

No one knows the true origin of this mysterious cocktail, but it started popping up in cocktail guides in the late 1940s as 'Mexico's El Diablo'.

- 60 ML (2 FL OZ/¼ CUP) TEQUILA
- 15 ML (½ FL OZ/1 TABLESPOON) CRÈME DE CASSIS
- 100 ML (3½ FL OZ/SCANT ½ CUP) GINGER BEER OR ENOUGH TO TOP UP

METHOD
Fill your highball glass with ice and pour in the tequila and ginger beer. Lastly, tip in the crème de cassis and serve.

GARNISH
Garnish with frozen blackberries and lime wheels.

SLOW MOVER

One to sit and watch the sunset with – sloe gin and tequila work really well together. The soda lifts the flavours of the sloe berries to the nose.

- 30 ML (1 FL OZ) TEQUILA
- 30 ML (1 FL OZ) SLOE GIN
- 75 ML (2½ FL OZ) SODA WATER (CLUB SODA), OR ENOUGH TO TOP UP

METHOD
Fill your tumbler glass with ice and pour in the tequila and sloe gin. Top with soda and serve.

GARNISH
Garnish with a cucumber peel spiral and orange peel.

TEQRONI

Like a Negroni but with tequila instead of gin. Teqroni is less bitter, smoother going down, and may be more palatable to people who find Negronis too strong.

- 30 ML (1 FL OZ) SILVER TEQUILA
- 30 ML (1 FL OZ) APEROL
- 30 ML (1 FL OZ) SWEET VERMOUTH

METHOD

Fill your tumbler glass with ice and set aside. Fill your shaker with ice and then pour in all the ingredients. Stir for 20 seconds and then strain into your glass and serve.

GARNISH

Garnish with a morello cherry.

TEQUILA SUNSET

The more mellow of the sisters, this uses Chambord instead of grenadine, which lifts and refines this drink, differentiating it from the syrupy Tequila Sunrise.

- 30 ML (1 FL OZ) CHAMBORD OR A RASPBERRY LIQUEUR
- 100 ML (3½ FL OZ/SCANT ½ CUP) PINEAPPLE JUICE
- 30 ML (1 FL OZ) REPOSADO TEQUILA

METHOD

Fill your highball glass with ice and pour in the Chambord, then the pineapple juice and finally the tequila. Give the cocktail a small stir and serve.

GARNISH

Garnish with a pineapple wedge and three raspberries.

SILVER BULLET

This beautifully smooth tequila martini is the perfect drink to enjoy after a long, stressful day.

- 60 ML (2 FL OZ/¼ CUP) SILVER TEQUILA
- 15 ML (½ FL OZ/1 TABLESPOON) GINGER SYRUP
- 15 ML (½ FL OZ/1 TABLESPOON) EXTRA-DRY VERMOUTH

METHOD
Fill a cocktail shaker with ice, then add all the ingredients. Secure the lid and shake vigorously for 20 seconds, then strain into your martini glass and serve.

GARNISH
Garnish with a slice of stem ginger.

LA PERLA

Calling all sherry lovers! This sophisticated cocktail was made just for you.

- 50 ML (1¾ FL OZ) REPOSADO TEQUILA
- 50 ML (1¾ FL OZ) MANZANILLA SHERRY
- 30 ML (1 FL OZ) CALVADOS

METHOD
Fill your shaker with ice then add all the ingredients. Stir for 20 seconds and then strain into your coupe glass and serve.

GARNISH
Garnish with slices of pear and a lemon twist.

MARGARITA

A classic three-ingredient cocktail, and, in my opinion, the best. This recipe calls for it to be served on the rocks – my own preferred order.

- 60 ML (2 FL OZ/¼ CUP) SILVER TEQUILA
- 30 ML (1 FL OZ) TRIPLE SEC OR GRAND MARNIER
- 30 ML (1 FL OZ) LIME JUICE

METHOD

Fill your margarita or tumbler glass with ice and set aside. Fill your cocktail shaker with ice and then add all of the ingredients. Secure the lid and shake vigorously for 20 seconds. Strain into your glass and serve.

GARNISH

Garnish with a slice of lime and give half the glass a salted rim.

SPARKLING RITA

Your guests will love this pretty bit of tequila fun in a glass. Super-quick and easy to prepare but still fancy and special. You should be able to find sparkling grapefruit (grapefruit soda) at most supermarkets.

> PICTURED ON PAGE 104 <

- 30 ML (1 FL OZ) REPOSADO TEQUILA
- 15 ML (½ FL OZ/1 TABLESPOON) COINTREAU
- 150 ML (5 FL OZ/SCANT 2/3 CUP) SPARKLING GRAPEFRUIT (GRAPEFRUIT SODA)

BATCH TO SERVE 4

- 120 ML (4 FL OZ/½ CUP) REPOSADO TEQUILA
- 60 ML (2 FL OZ/¼ CUP) COINTREAU
- 600 ML (20 FL OZ/2½ CUPS) SPARKLING GRAPEFRUIT (GRAPEFRUIT SODA)

METHOD

Fill your tumbler glass with ice and pour in the tequila and Cointreau. Top with the grapefruit soda, stir and serve. If you are making a batch, put all of the ingredients in a jug (pitcher) or punch bowl with ice, stir and serve.

GARNISH

Garnish with candied orange and lemons.

TEQUILA SNACKS

⇉⟶

I love tequila cocktails because they make me as happy as really good bar food does. Hanging out with friends, drinking Margaritas and eating big platters of messy food is my perfect evening. So forget jostling for good seats and waiting for service and bring the best parts of the bar home. The snacks here are for sharing with friends and family who leave pretension at the door.

VEGAN | SERVES 6

HOT CAULIFLOWER WINGS WITH BLUE CHEESE DIP

Guilt-free hot wings! These vegan bites are just as good as their meat counterpart. They are simple to make, baked not fried, and there are no pesky bones to deal with.

45 MINS

INGREDIENTS

- 125 G (4 OZ/1 CUP) PLAIN (ALL-PURPOSE) FLOUR
- 1 TABLESPOON SMOKED PAPRIKA
- 200 ML (7 FL OZ/SCANT 1 CUP) ALMOND MILK
- 1 CAULIFLOWER, BROKEN INTO ROUGHLY 5-CM (2-IN) FLORETS
- 100 ML (3½ FL OZ/SCANT ½ CUP) HOT SAUCE
- 1 TABLESPOON VEGETABLE OIL

BLUE CHEESE DIP

- 2 TABLESPOONS CREAM CHEESE
- 3 TABLESPOONS SOUR CREAM
- 2 TABLESPOONS WHITE WINE VINEGAR
- 120 G (3¾ OZ) BLUE CHEESE
- SALT

METHOD

Heat the oven to 220°C (430°F/gas 8). Line a lipped baking sheet (pan) with non-stick baking parchment. In a large bowl, mix the flour with the paprika, almond milk and a large pinch of salt until you get a smooth batter – you may not need all the almond milk. Add the florets and mix well until each floret is evenly coated.

Using a spoon or tongs, remove the florets from the batter and lay them out evenly, in a single layer, across the baking sheet, leaving the excess batter in the bowl. Bake for 10 minutes, then turn over each floret and bake for another 10 minutes.

Meanwhile, mix the hot sauce with the oil in a small bowl. Next, make the blue cheese dip. In a small bowl mix the cream cheese with the sour cream, vinegar and a large pinch of salt. Crumble in the blue cheese, mix well and set aside until serving.

After the initial 20 minutes of baking, spoon over or brush the hot sauce mixture onto each floret and then return to the oven to bake for another 15 minutes. Serve straight away with the dipping sauce on the side.

VEGAN | MAKES 16

CORNBREAD TOPPED WITH PICKLED RED ONION, AVOCADO & POMEGRANATE SEEDS

Make the cornbread ahead and pop the toppings on just before your guests arrive. Or cut into 4 pieces and serve for lunch.

30 MINS (PLUS COOLING)

INGREDIENTS

- 150 G (5 OZ/1 CUP) POLENTA (CORNMEAL)
- 125 G (4 OZ/1 CUP) PLAIN (ALL-PURPOSE) FLOUR
- 50 G (2 OZ/¼ CUP) CASTER (GRANULATED) SUGAR
- 2 TEASPOONS BAKING POWDER
- ½ TEASPOON SALT
- 100 G (3 ½ OZ) SWEETCORN (CORN KERNELS)
- 250 ML (8 ½ FL OZ/1 CUP) ALMOND MILK
- 100 ML (3 ½ FL OZ/SCANT ½ CUP) VEGETABLE OIL
- ½ SMALL RED ONION, THINLY SLICED
- 2 TABLESPOONS RED WINE VINEGAR
- 1 AVOCADO, SLICED
- A HANDFUL OF POMEGRANATE SEEDS

METHOD

Heat oven to 200°C (400°F/gas 6). Line a 20-cm (8-in) square pan with baking parchment. In a large bowl, add the polenta, flour, sugar, baking powder and salt. Mix the ingredients together. Pour in the almond milk, sweetcorn and the vegetable oil and combine until you have a smooth mixture. Pour into the lined pan and put into the oven. Bake for 20 minutes or until risen, golden and cracked. Leave to cool.

Meanwhile, mix the red onion with the red wine vinegar. Leave to sit for 10 minutes and then drain.

Cut the cornbread into 16 squares. Put onto a serving plate and top each with slices of avocado, red onion and a sprinkling of pomegranate seeds.

SERVES 6

LOADED BEEF NACHOS

I don't think I could be friends with someone who doesn't like nachos. What's not to like: tortilla chips, melted cheese and every topping under the sun!

INGREDIENTS

- OLIVE OIL
- 400 G (14 OZ) BEEF MINCE (GROUND BEEF)
- ½ TEASPOON GARLIC GRANULES
- ½ TEASPOON CHILLI POWDER
- 1 TABLESPOON TOMATO PURÉE (PASTE)
- 3 TABLESPOONS SOUR CREAM
- 3 TABLESPOONS CREAM CHEESE
- 1 BAG OF TORTILLA CHIPS
- 150 G (5 OZ) CHEDDAR OR MONTEREY JACK, GRATED
- 3 TABLESPOONS JALAPEÑO PEPPER SLICES FROM A JAR
- 150 G (5 OZ) CHERRY TOMATOES, QUARTERED
- 3 TABLESPOONS SLICED BLACK OLIVES
- 1 AVOCADO, CHOPPED
- 1 LIME, ZESTED AND JUICED
- A HANDFUL OF CORIANDER (CILANTRO) LEAVES
- SALT

METHOD

Heat a drizzle of olive oil in a pan and add the beef. Cook until broken up and browned. Add the garlic granules, chilli powder and tomato purée and cook for a further 5 minutes on a medium heat, then set aside.

Heat the oven to 200°C (400°F/gas 6). Mix the sour cream with the cream cheese and set aside. In a large baking dish, arrange two layers of chips with the beef, grated cheese and jalapeño slices. Bake for 15 minutes or until the cheese has melted. Meanwhile make the salsa by mixing the tomatoes in a bowl with the black olives, avocado, lime zest and juice and a pinch of salt. Remove the nachos from the oven and top with the sour cream mix and salsa and then scatter over the coriander and serve.

WHISKEY

Very broadly speaking, there are three types of whiskey and two spellings. Whiskey with an 'e' is from Ireland and the United States, and whisky without an 'e' is from Scotland, Canada or Japan. Whisky cannot be called 'Scotch' unless it is produced and bottled in Scotland. The three types are whiskey, rye and bourbon. Whiskey has a smokey flavour, rye is spicy and bourbon is sweet. There's a lot more to it than that, but this small amount of knowledge will be enough to impress your guests. But to truly know whiskey would take a lifetime of research/drinking.

OLD-FASHIONED

'Cocktail' was first used to mean a spirit, sugar and bitters. And that's exactly what's in an Old-Fashioned, the granddaddy of cocktails.

- 60 ML (2 FL OZ/¼ CUP) BOURBON WHISKEY
- 1 SUGAR CUBE
- 3 DASHES OF ANGOSTURA BITTERS

METHOD

Muddle the sugar and bitters into a paste in your tumbler glass. Add the bourbon and stir until the sugar has nearly dissolved. Add ice and continue to stir for 30 seconds and then serve.

GARNISH

Garnish with a thick orange twist.

DRUNK UNCLE

You're probably unfamiliar with this cocktail but it's more popular that you think and may just be your next order at the bar. Though similar-sounding to a Negroni (see page 52), this is very much its own drink with a luscious, smokey flavour. Be sure to use a bianco rather than a dry vermouth – bianco is sweet and will give this cocktail the balance it needs.

- 60 ML (2 FL OZ/¼ CUP) WHISKEY
- 30 ML (1 FL OZ) CYNAR AMARO OR CAMPARI
- 30 ML (1 FL OZ) VERMOUTH BIANCO

METHOD
Fill a shaker with ice and pour in all the ingredients. Stir for 20 seconds and then strain into your glass and serve over ice.

GARNISH
Garnish with a slice of grapefruit.

HIDDEN ORCHARD

Perfect for an autumnal gathering such as a Bonfire Night or Halloween party.

> PICTURED ON PAGE 129 <

- 30 ML (1 FL OZ) BOURBON WHISKEY
- 30 ML (1 FL OZ) CLOUDY APPLE JUICE
- 100 ML (3½ FL OZ/SCANT ½ CUP) DRY GINGER ALE, OR ENOUGH TO TOP UP

BATCH TO SERVE 4

- 100 ML (3½ FL OZ/SCANT ½ CUP) BOURBON WHISKEY
- 100 ML (3½ FL OZ/SCANT ½ CUP) CLOUDY APPLE JUICE
- 400 ML (13 FL OZ/GENEROUS 1½ CUPS) DRY GINGER ALE

METHOD

Fill your Mason jar or tumbler glass with ice and pour in the bourbon and apple juice. Top with dry ginger ale, stir and serve.

If making the batch in a punch bowl, add a few handfuls of ice to the bowl, pour in the ingredients, give it a stir and have your guests help themselves.

GARNISH

Garnish with apple slices and toffee sweets (candies).

MINT JULEP

This may be the signature drink of the Kentucky Derby, but you can drink it any time! So easy to make and incredibly delicious, the fresh mint and bourbon combination is one of my favourites.

- 60 ML (2 FL OZ/¼ CUP) BOURBON WHISKEY
- 10 MINT LEAVES
- 15 ML (½ FL OZ) 1 TABLESPOON SIMPLE SUGAR SYRUP

METHOD

Put the mint and syrup in your highball glass and muddle them for 20 seconds. Add the bourbon. Fill your glass with crushed ice and stir well for 20 seconds. Top up with more crushed ice and serve.

GARNISH
Garnish with sprigs of mint.

MONTE CARLO

A sweeter and smoother variation on the Manhattan (see page 118).

- 60 ML (2 FL OZ/¼ CUP) RYE WHISKEY
- 30 ML (1 FL OZ) BENEDICTINE LIQUEUR
- 2 DASHES OF ANGOSTURA BITTERS

METHOD

Fill your tumbler glass with ice and set aside. Fill a shaker with ice and pour in all the ingredients. Stir for 20 seconds and then strain into a glass and serve.

GARNISH
Garnish with a large strip of lemon rind.

MANHATTAN

The timeless whiskey cocktail. This drink embodies the style and grace of the 1950s. It has a depth to its flavour and a light, slightly sweet finish.

- 60 ML (2 FL OZ/¼ CUP) RYE WHISKEY
- 30 ML (1 FL OZ) SWEET VERMOUTH
- 2 DASHES OF ANGOSTURA BITTERS

METHOD

Fill a shaker with ice and pour in all the ingredients. Stir for 20 seconds then strain into your martini glass and serve.

GARNISH

Garnish with a morello cherry.

REVOLVER

Another spin on a Manhattan, this time with a kick of caffeine!

- 60 ML (2 FL OZ/¼ CUP) BOURBON WHISKEY
- 30 ML (1 FL OZ) KAHLUA
- 2 DASHES OF ANGOSTURA BITTERS

METHOD

Fill a shaker with ice and pour in all the ingredients. Stir for 20 seconds, then strain into your coupe glass and serve.

GARNISH

Garnish with an orange twist.

RICKEY

This is the original Rickey cocktail, named after a 19th-century American politician who had a penchant for cocktails but didn't like sugar. The bartender at his local knew this so one day added lime to Joe Rickey's usual order of a bourbon and soda and the Rickey was born, greatly outshining the man himself in fame (much to his displeasure).

- 60 ML (2 FL OZ/¼ CUP) BOURBON WHISKEY

- ½ A LIME

- 100 ML (3½ FL OZ/SCANT ½ CUP) SODA WATER (CLUB SODA),OR ENOUGH TO TOP UP

METHOD

Fill your highball glass with ice, pour in the bourbon and then squeeze in the juice of half a lime, dropping the lime into the glass once finished. Top up with soda, stir and serve.

GARNISH

Garnish with half a lime.

WHISKEY SOUR

One of the few, maybe the only sour to be made without egg white – delicious!

- 60 ML (2 FL OZ/¼ CUP) BOURBON WHISKEY
- 30 ML (1 FL OZ) LEMON JUICE
- 30 ML (1 FL OZ) SIMPLE SUGAR SYRUP

METHOD

Fill your tumbler glass with ice and set aside. Fill a shaker with ice and pour in all the ingredients. Stir for 20 seconds and then strain into your glass and serve.

GARNISH

Garnish with a maraschino cherry and a twist of lemon.

WHISKEY SPRITZ

This is a great cocktail if you like the flavour of whiskey but find it too harsh to drink straight. The soda takes the bite away, leaving a smooth finish.

- 60 ML (2 FL OZ/¼ CUP) WHISKEY
- 3 DASHES OF ANGOSTURA BITTERS
- 100 ML SODA WATER (CLUB SODA), OR ENOUGH TO TOP UP

METHOD

Fill your highball glass with ice and pour in the whiskey and add the bitters. Top up with soda, stir and serve.

GARNISH

Garnish with a twist of lemon.

WHISKEY SNACKS

→

Bold, strong flavours are often served with whiskey, such as smoked fish, roasted meats and pungent cheeses, but because there are so many different kinds of whiskey, offering such a variety of flavours, you could probably find a whiskey to match any dish! Because of this it's becoming more popular to serve with food, from light starters to indulgent desserts. The snacks I have included will greatly complement the chapter's variety of cocktails, like the roasted cured sausage with a fiery bitter glaze, a fresh and light creamy dip, and everyone's favourite – a baked wheel of stinky cheese!

SERVES 4

BAKED SALAMI WITH MARMALADE & MUSTARD

This is a favourite of my family back home in Toronto. This dish has been around for years but is rarely served these days. I want to bring it back to the main stage!

45 MINS

INGREDIENTS

- 1 WHOLE SALAMI, ABOUT 200 G (7 OZ)
- 1 TABLESPOON DRY ENGLISH MUSTARD POWDER
- 3 TABLESPOONS MARMALADE
- ENGLISH MUSTARD, TO SERVE

METHOD

Heat the oven to 180°C (350°F/gas 4). Cut a criss-cross pattern into the salami, slicing all the way to the bottom of the sausage without cutting through the bottom casing. In a baking pan, put a layer of kitchen foil. Put the salami in the middle of the kitchen foil and sprinkle over the dry mustard powder. Spoon over the marmalade, ensuring it goes into all the cuts and leaving some to sit on top. Bring up the sides of the kitchen foil and loosely seal the edges by scrunching them together over the top of the salami. Bake for 40 minutes.

Serve on a platter with a knife. Cut off some of the slices and spear with cocktail sticks (toothpicks) and leave the rest for your guests to spear for themselves. Serve with English mustard.

VEGETARIAN

BAKED CAMEMBERT WITH HAZELNUTS, ROSEMARY & GARLIC

So easy, so quick, so delicious. Using the microwave melts the cheese in seconds. If you don't have a microwave it will take longer, but it will be just as good in the oven.

5 MINS

INGREDIENTS

- 1 TABLESPOON OLIVE OIL
- 3 TABLESPOONS BLANCHED HAZELNUTS, ROUGHLY CHOPPED
- 1 SPRIG OF ROSEMARY, LEAVES PICKED AND ROUGHLY CHOPPED
- 1 GARLIC CLOVE, SLICED
- A PINCH OF SUGAR
- 250 G (9 OZ) WHEEL OF CAMEMBERT, ALL PACKAGING REMOVED

TO SERVE

- CRUSTY BREAD (I USED HONEY, ALMOND AND WALNUT BREAD)

METHOD

Heat the oil in a pan. Add the nuts, rosemary, garlic and sugar and cook until the garlic is golden.

Using a large knife, carefully cut off the top rind of the Camembert and discard. Put the Camembert in the centre of a serving plate that is microwave-safe. Microwave for 50 seconds or until the cheese has started to melt over the side. Remove from the microwave and spoon over the hazelnut mixture. Serve straight away, with bread.

SERVES 6

HOT CRAB DIP

Crab dip is a staple on party menus back home in Canada. The fresh-ocean flavour of the crab mixed with the spices and silkiness of the cheese make it irresistible. If you can get fresh crab meat, wonderful, but if not, don't fret, canned crab works fabulously.

35 MINS

INGREDIENTS

- 150 G (5 OZ) CREAM CHEESE
- 50 G (2 OZ) SOUR CREAM
- 200 G (7 OZ) WHITE CRAB MEAT OR 2 X 170-G (6-OZ) TINS OF CRAB MEAT, DRAINED
- 1 SHALLOT, FINELY CHOPPED
- 1 TEASPOON LEMON JUICE
- ¼ TEASPOON CAYENNE PEPPER
- ½ TEASPOON WORCESTERSHIRE SAUCE
- 2 TABLESPOONS GRATED PARMESAN

TO SERVE

- CRUDITÉS OF YOUR CHOICE
- TOASTED BAGUETTE SLICES

METHOD

Heat the oven to 200°C (400°F/gas 6). In a large bowl, mix all the ingredients together. Pour into a baking dish (I used a 18 x 4 cm (7 x 1^1/2 in) terracotta one) and put in the top third of the oven for 30 minutes until bubbling at the sides and starting to brown. Serve straight from the oven with your favourite raw veg and/or lightly toasted baguette.

SPARKLING

Champagne, prosecco and cava are all drunk neat and unaltered traditionally, or, if you're having Christmas with the in-laws, maybe as a Bucks Fizz. But here are 10 recipes that demonstrate how versatile and delicious sparkling wine cocktails can be – always perfect for any scale of celebration, or just an elaborate hair of the dog! Don't worry about vintage labels or high price-tags, find a bottle of bubbles that you enjoy, that doesn't cost the earth, and get creative.

CHAMPAGNE COCKTAIL

This is aptly named 'Champagne Cocktail' because it is, in fact, the classic Champagne Cocktail. In the original recipe there is a sugar cube added to the glass as well, but using a sweet brandy works just fine.

- 30 ML (1 FL OZ) BRANDY
- 2 DASHES OF ANGOSTURA BITTERS
- CHAMPAGNE TO TOP UP

METHOD

Pour the brandy into your coupe or flute, add the bitters, top up with Champagne and serve.

GARNISH

Garnish with a sugared rim.

APEROL SPRITZ

This is a well-loved classic that never gets old.

- 60 ML (2 FL OZ/¼ CUP) APEROL
- 90 ML (3 FL OZ) PROSECCO
- 30 ML (1 FL OZ) SODA WATER (CLUB SODA)

METHOD

Add a handful of ice to your large wine glass. Pour the Aperol, prosecco and soda into your glass and serve.

GARNISH

Garnish with a slice of orange.

VALENTINA

A sexy little number – the tropical flavour of rum complements the biscuity taste of Champagne, with the strawberries adding the sweet, fresh aromas of summer to this delightful cocktail.

- 30 ML (1 FL OZ) WHITE RUM
- 1 STRAWBERRY, HALVED
- PINK CHAMPAGNE TO TOP UP

METHOD

Pour the rum into your glass. Add the strawberries, top up with the pink Champagne and serve.

GARNISH

Garnish with a slice of strawberry.

BOMBSHELL

This cocktail will get the fizz-haters out there changing their tune. The grapefruit juice adds strong notes of tart citrus, and the syrupy grenadine rounds off the flavour for a balanced and refreshing drink.

- 60 ML (2 FL OZ/¼ CUP) GRAPEFRUIT JUICE
- DRY SPARKLING WINE TO TOP UP
- 15 ML (½ FL OZ/1 TABLESPOON) GRENADINE

BATCH TO SERVE 6

- 400 ML (13 FL OZ/GENEROUS 1½ CUPS) GRAPEFRUIT JUICE
- DRY SPARKLING WINE TO TOP UP
- 100 ML (3½ FL OZ/SCANT ½ CUP) GRENADINE

METHOD

Fill your highball glass with ice and pour in the grapefruit juice and grenadine. Top up with sparkling wine, give it a stir and serve.

For a batch, fill individual glasses with ice and then make the cocktail in a large pouring jug (pitcher) or punch bowl with ladle (a couple handfuls of ice in the bowl) and serve.

GARNISH
Garnish with strawberries.

GREEN GOBLIN

Chartreuse has a strong flavour that's not for everyone, but if you like Pernod and ouzo then this is the Champagne cocktail for you.

- 30 ML (1 FL OZ) LIME JUICE
- 30 ML (1 FL OZ) CHARTREUSE
- CHAMPAGNE TO TOP UP

METHOD
Fill your tumbler glass with ice, pour in the lime juice and Chartreuse and stir to combine. Top up with Champagne and serve.

GARNISH
Garnish with fresh herbs such as mint, rosemary and thyme.

SPANISH 75

This is based on the original French 75 created at Harry's New York Bar in Paris during WWI, but I've used cava instead of Champagne as it's slightly sweeter, and left out the sugar.

> PICTURED ON PAGE 151 <

- 30 ML (1 FL OZ) GIN
- 15 ML (½ FL OZ/1 TABLESPOON) LEMON JUICE
- CAVA TO TOP UP

METHOD
Pour the gin and the lemon juice into your flute glass. Top up with cava and serve.

GARNISH
Garnish with a twist of lemon.

RITZ FIZZ

The Ritz-Carlton hotel created this cocktail to celebrate the end of prohibition in the United States.

- 15 ML (½ FL OZ/1 TABLESPOON) AMARETTO LIQUEUR
- 15 ML (½ FL OZ/1 TABLESPOON) BLUE CURAÇAO
- CHAMPAGNE TO TOP UP

METHOD

Add a large handful of ice to a cocktail shaker, pour in the amaretto and blue curaçao and shake vigorously for 20 seconds. Strain into your flute glass, top up with Champagne and serve.

GARNISH

Garnish with a slice of lemon in the glass.

CHERRY MIMOSA

The Champagne and orange juice measurements depend on the size of your glass. The usual rule for a mimosa is half sparking and half juice. The kirsch adds a depth of flavour that you probably won't have realised you have been missing all along!

- ORANGE JUICE
- CHAMPAGNE
- 15 ML (½ FL OZ/1 TABLESPOON) KIRSCH

METHOD

Almost half-fill flute or coupe glass with orange juice. Pour in the same amount of Champagne. Finish by adding the kirsch and serve.

GARNISH

Garnish with a morello cherry.

TURKISH DELIGHT

An absolutely beautiful cocktail that will take you to a far away land of exotic pleasures.

- 1 TEASPOON CASTER (GRANULATED) SUGAR
- 1 TEASPOON ROSEWATER
- CAVA TO TOP UP

METHOD

Firstly, put the sugar in your flute or coupe glass. Add a little cava and stir for 20 seconds or until the sugar has dissolved. Pour more cava into the glass until it's three quarters full, then add the rosewater and serve.

GARNISH

Garnish with a dried rose petal or a slice of Turkish delight.

NUTTY BELLINI

I associate both Bellinis and almond-flavoured treats with Italy, and I love all things Italian, so this is my perfect cocktail

> PICTURED ON PAGE 148 <

- 15 ML (½ FL OZ/1 TABLESPOON) AMARETTO LIQUEUR
- 30 ML (1 FL OZ) PEACH JUICE
- PROSECCO, TO TOP UP

METHOD

Pour the peach juice into your flute. Add prosecco to three quarter-fill the flute. Add the amaretto, stir gently with a spoon and serve.

GARNISH

Garnish with a slice of peach.

SPARKLING SNACKS

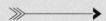

Workers in the wine trade, especially those specialising in bubbles, implore you to pair food with your glasses of fizz. Sparkling wines go with food just as well as still wines. From fish and chips to game to fruity desserts, there's always bottle of bubbly to match. The snacks I've included here are perfect for when you want to push the boat out and have your cooking look a bit fancy but don't want to spend all your time in the kitchen.

CHICORY WITH SMOKED SALMON, DILL CRÈME FRAÎCHE & CAPERS

This easy and quick-to-make dish is a family favourite that your guests will want the recipe for so they can make it themselves at their next party.

10 MINS

INGREDIENTS

- 200 G (7 OZ) CRÈME FRAÎCHE
- 1 HEAPED TABLESPOON ROUGHLY CHOPPED DILL
- 2 HEADS OF WHITE CHICORY (ENDIVE), LEAVES PULLED APART
- 300 G (10½ OZ) SMOKED SALMON
- 3 HEAPED TABLESPOONS CAPERS
- 1 LEMON, CUT INTO WEDGES
- BLACK PEPPER

METHOD

In a small bowl, mix the crème fraîche with the dill and a few grinds of black pepper. Lay out the chicory leaves on a serving plate. Spread a dollop of the crème fraîche sauce in each chicory leaf. Divide the salmon between the leaves, laying them on top of the sauce. Top each leaf with 3 or 4 capers. Squeeze over a couple of wedges of lemon and serve.

MAKES 12

MINI-YORKSHIRE PUD, STEAK & HORSERADISH PARMESAN CREAM WITH ROCKET & SHAVED PARMESAN

40 MINS

Everyone's favourite – and it's simple! The most effort involved here is buying a mini-muffin pan. Using steak is a cheat's way of getting around the stress and drama of perfectly roasting beef.

Heat the oven to 220°C (430°F/gas 8). To make the batter, put the flour and a pinch of salt in a measuring jug (pitcher). Crack in the eggs and, using a fork, mix to a smooth paste. Add the milk in stages, mixing until smooth between each pour. Allow to rest for 10 minutes.

Using a 12-hole mini-muffin pan, pour about 1 teaspoon of oil into each hole, then put the pan in the oven for 5 minutes to get really hot. Remove the pan from the oven and pour the batter into each hole. Bake for 12 minutes or until risen and golden. Remove from the pan to cool completely.

Make the horseradish cream in a small bowl. Mix the horseradish sauce with the crème fraîche and set aside.

To cook the steak, heat about 1 tablespoon of oil in a frying pan (skillet) over a high heat until hot. Sprinkle a pinch of salt and a few gratings of pepper over each side of the steak, and then add to the pan. Cook for 2 minutes on each side and then remove from the pan and rest for 5 minutes. Remove any hard fat from the edges. Cut the steak into 5-mm (1/4-in) slices, lengthways, down the steak, so you get long strips.

To assemble, put the puds on a serving dish. Add a dollop of the horseradish cream to each. Loosely roll up the slices of steak and poke them into the cream. Sprinkle the rocket (arugala) leaves and Parmesan curls over the puds, and serve.

INGREDIENTS

- 120 G (4 ¼ OZ/ SCANT 1 CUP) PLAIN (ALL-PURPOSE) FLOUR
- 2 EGGS
- 100 ML (7 FL OZ/ SCANT 1 CUP) MILK
- SUNFLOWER OIL
- 200 G (7 OZ) SIRLOIN STEAK
- 3 TABLESPOONS HORSERADISH SAUCE
- 2 TABLESPOONS CRÈME FRAÎCHE
- 2 HANDFULS OF ROCKET (ARUGULA)
- 12 SHAVINGS OF PARMESAN
- SALT
- BLACK PEPPER

VEGAN | MAKES 24

MAPLE GARLIC CHESTNUT PÂTÉ & ROASTED PEAR CROSTINI

Toast your baguette slices, make the pâté and have your bowl of spiced pears, ready-to-roast in advance, to maximise the time you'll have to socialise. This vegan-friendly starter will have even the meat-eaters coming back for more.

INGREDIENTS

- 1 BAGUETTE CUT INTO 1.5-CM (³/₄-IN) SLICES
- 180 G (6¼ OZ) COOKED CHESTNUTS
- 1 SMALL GARLIC CLOVE
- 1 TABLESPOON MAPLE SYRUP
- A PINCH OF GROUND NUTMEG
- 3 RED PEARS, SLICED, PEELED AND CORED
- 1 TABLESPOON OLIVE OIL
- ½ TEASPOON GROUND GINGER
- 2 TABLESPOONS THYME LEAVES
- SALT
- BLACK PEPPER

METHOD

Heat the oven to 200°C (400°F/gas 6). Lay out the slices of baguette on a baking sheet and put them into the oven for 5 minutes or until lightly toasted. Set aside on a serving dish.

Make the chestnut pâté using a food processor or hand blender. Add the chestnuts, garlic, maple syrup, nutmeg, ¼ teaspoon salt and 2 tablespoons water to the bowl. Whizz for about 30 seconds or until you have a smooth paste.

In a large bowl, mix the pear slices with the olive oil, ginger, thyme and a pinch of salt and a couple of grinds of black pepper. Tip out and spread them evenly across a lipped baking sheet lined with baking parchment. Roast in the oven for 10 minutes.

Meanwhile, spread the chestnut pâté on the toasted baguette. Once out of the oven, using a fork, top each crostini with a few slices of roasted pear, then serve.

INDEX

ABOUT THE AUTHOR

Kate Calder is a recipe writer and food stylist with more than a decade's worth of experience in the kitchens of BBC GoodFood, Olive and Good Housekeeping. Hailing from Canada, but now based in London with her young family, Kate's passion for food led her away from her previous career in the film industry.

ACKNOWLEDGEMENTS

The opportunity to create this book went a long way in offsetting the trials and tribulations of 2020, the toughest of which was feeling so far away from Canada and my family. It has been an absolute joy to make and that's down to the many people who helped me do it. Massive thank yous to all my amazing friends and family who listened to my ideas, advised, brainstormed cocktail names, tested recipes, and gave me unwavering encouragement and support.

Growing up in downtown Toronto made me a foodie before the term had even been coined. Our family regularly dined in restaurants, greasy spoons to fine dining, if it tasted good the Calder's had booked a table for 4. And then there's my parents' hosting skills - they know how to throw a great cocktail party! Excellent chat, too much food, too much drink and a fantastic playlist has always made the end of Walker Avenue the house party to be at. Thank you mom and dad for sharing your love of food and entertaining with me and Tess. Even more importantly thank you for always encouraging me to chase after my dreams and to be open and friendly while doing it.

To my sister Tess and brother-in-law Pauly in Australia, thank you for pickling your garden's goods for me and always bringing the fun, laughter and love into the room.

To my neighbours, thank you for being my taste testers and giving me great feedback.

Jonny Muir, world's greatest Manny and a triple threat. My family adores you. There's no way I could have found the time to do this book if it wasn't for you and your incredible energy.

Max and Liz Haarala Hamilton, the kindest and most talented team. This shoot was such a fun, positive experience after a very hard year. It truly was one of the best weeks of my life. Thank you for having me in your world and making every photo more beautiful than I could have imagined.

Jen Kay, what a master of beauty you are! You brought the beauty, style, elegance and fun that I wished for.

Thank you to my assistant Peter Sandys-Clarke for taking time out from in front of the camera to be my rock in the kitchen, and for the cocktail garnish marmalade - delicious.

Julia Murray, thank you for your absolutely beautiful illustrations and stunning design. I want to frame every single thing you've ever drawn for this book.

To my adorable, clever rascals, thank you Sonny for helping me come up with so many cocktail ideas and to you and Bo for suffering my many garnish attempts on your cups of water.

Thank you to Ben for getting drunk with me day after day and still managing to change dirty nappies in-between sips. And also for being my biggest champion for the last 21 years.

And finally the biggest thank you and bear hug goes to my editor and friend Eve Marleau. This book happened because of your belief in me and your incredibly chilled and nurturing soul. Thank you for answering my endless questions and not minding that I sometimes swear a lot. I love you!

PUBLISHED IN 2021 BY HARDIE GRANT BOOKS,
AN IMPRINT OF HARDIE GRANT PUBLISHING

HARDIE GRANT BOOKS (LONDON)
5TH & 6TH FLOORS
52–54 SOUTHWARK STREET
LONDON SE1 1UN

HARDIE GRANT BOOKS (MELBOURNE)
BUILDING 1, 658 CHURCH STREET
RICHMOND, VICTORIA 3121

HARDIEGRANTBOOKS.COM

BRITISH LIBRARY CATALOGUING-IN-PUBLICATION DATA. A CATALOGUE RECORD FOR THIS BOOK
IS AVAILABLE FROM THE BRITISH LIBRARY.

THREE INGREDIENT COCKTAILS BY KATE CALDER
ISBN: 978-1-78488-471-0

10 9 8 7 6 5 4 3 2 1

PUBLISHER: KAJAL MISTRY
COMMISSIONING EDITOR: EVE MARLEAU
DESIGN AND ILLUSTRATION: JULIA MURRAY
PHOTOGRAPHER: HAARALA HAMILTON
PROP STYLIST: JENNIFER KAY
COPY-EDITOR: GREGOR SHEPHERD
PROOFREADER: GILLIAN HASLAM
INDEXER: VANESSA BIRD
PRODUCTION CONTROLLER: NIKOLAUS GINELLI

COLOUR REPRODUCTION BY P2D
PRINTED AND BOUND IN CHINA BY LEO PAPER PRODUCTS LTD.